CONTENTS

CANDLEWICK PRESS
CAMBRIDGE, MASSACHUSETTS

HIGH IN THE SKY

Steve Parker

1 People have always dreamed of flying, but it was only just over 200 years ago that they succeeded — on November 21, 1783.

2 A few months earlier, in Paris, Joseph and Étienne Montgolfier had a brilliant idea. The brothers made a balloon-shaped bag and held it over a fire. When they let go, hot air from the fire carried the bag upward.

3 Would a huge balloon full of hot air lift people into the sky? they wondered. And if it did, would there be air to breathe that far above the ground?

4 To experiment, the brothers made a bigger balloon and sent it up carrying a sheep, a duck, and a rooster in a hamper. The animals survived!

5 The balloon that carried the first human passengers was even larger, and inside its base there was a fire in a metal basket. On that famous November day, two volunteers, Pilâtre de Rozier and the Marquis d'Arlandes, climbed aboard.

The crowd cheered when the balloon rose into the sky. The two brave travelers fed the fire with straw as the balloon drifted for 25 minutes across Paris. The Age of Flight had begun!

2 HOT-AIR BALLOONS

UP, UP AND AWAY

1 Can you imagine blowing up a balloon that's taller than a house? Hot-air balloons are huge — the balloon part is called the canopy, and it can be 80 feet high!

2 If you opened out the canopy and laid it flat, it would cover four tennis courts. It's made of long panels of rip-proof nylon stitched together with more than 3 miles of thread.

3 The pilot and passengers ride inside a wicker basket. It's like a picnic basket, but much bigger, thicker, and sturdier.

4 Wicker is very strong, but also very light. All parts of the balloon have to be as light as possible because the only thing keeping the balloon up in the sky is . . .

5 hot air! The special thing about hot air is that it floats upward. You've seen this happen if you've ever watched smoke rising above a bonfire.

6 Hot-air balloons have burners at the mouth of their canopy, where gas is burned to heat the air. The hot air rushes into the canopy and pushes it upward, lifting the basket.

7 The gas fuel comes from bottles inside the basket. A dial shows how full the bottles are so that the pilot can land safely before the fuel runs out.

4 HOT-AIR BALLOONS

8 The pilot can land the balloon by letting some hot air out of an opening near the top of the canopy. With less hot air to hold it up, the balloon sinks slowly toward the ground.

9 A hot-air balloon can be made to go up or down, but there's no way to steer it — it simply drifts wherever the wind blows it.

10 That's why balloon flights are so exciting, though. You never know whose house you'll fly over or where you're going to land!

HOT-AIR BALLOONS 5

SHIPS IN THE SKY

1 Is it a balloon?
Is it a plane?
No, it's a bit of both —
an airship, or blimp.

2 Airships float like balloons, but they don't use hot air. The balloon part is called the envelope, and it's filled with a very light gas called helium.

3 Balloons drift with the wind, but airships don't. Like airplanes, they have engines to power them along.

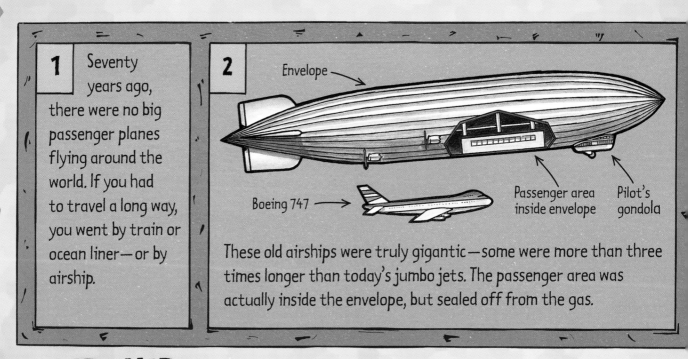

1 Seventy years ago, there were no big passenger planes flying around the world. If you had to travel a long way, you went by train or ocean liner—or by airship.

2 Envelope

Boeing 747

Passenger area inside envelope

Pilot's gondola

These old airships were truly gigantic—some were more than three times longer than today's jumbo jets. The passenger area was actually inside the envelope, but sealed off from the gas.

6 AIRSHIPS

4 This airship's engines are on either side of the back of the gondola. This is the cabin under the envelope, and it's where the passengers and pilot ride.

5 Although airships have engines, they can't fly very fast. So they're mainly used for things like sightseeing — when people want to travel slowly and quietly — and advertising.

3 The passenger area was like a hotel. You could listen to a piano player in the lounge, eat a meal in the dining room, or snooze in your own bedroom.

Bedrooms

Dining room

Lounge

4 But in those days, airships were filled with hydrogen. And unlike helium, this gas catches fire easily. By the late 1930s, several airships had blown up, killing hundreds of people. No one would risk flying in them, and the age of giant airships came to an end.

1 Flying a stunt plane is like riding the world's best roller coaster, but you're in charge!

Joystick →

Rudder pedals →

2 Press one of the pedals. The rudder flap on the tail fin moves, turning the plane sideways. Niaawoow, you're swinging around.

3 Push the joystick to one side and hold it there. Aileron flaps on the main wings move, and — ooooooohh — you're rolling right over.

4 Now pull the joystick toward you. Elevator flaps on the tail wings tilt up, pushing the plane's tail down and its nose up. Wheeeeeee, you're zooming upward.

5 Keep the joystick pulled back. You're looping up and right over — aaaaargh, where's the sick bag!

1 Why is this airplane upside down? It's a stunt plane for doing special displays, twisting and looping around in the sky. In a second, it'll turn right-side up again!

2 It's also a biplane, which means it has two pairs of wings. (Most planes are monoplanes, with just one pair.)

3 All airplanes have wings. They couldn't fly without them because wings keep a plane up in the air.

8 WINGED FLIGHT

WONDER WINGS

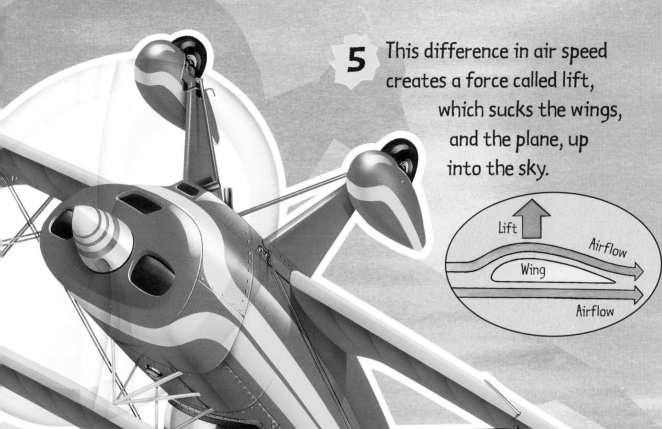

5 This difference in air speed creates a force called lift, which sucks the wings, and the plane, up into the sky.

Lift

Airflow

Wing

Airflow

4 Plane wings do this because they have a special shape — curved on top and flat underneath — which makes the airflow faster above them than below.

6 And it isn't hard to figure out that with two pairs of wings, biplanes have around twice as much lift!

WINGED FLIGHT 9

ROCKETING ALONG

1 Back in 1947, this airplane was the fastest thing on wings. It was called the Bell X-1, and it had the most powerful kind of engine in the world — a rocket.

2 The Bell X-1 was designed for just one job. It was to be the first plane to go supersonic — that means to travel faster than sound . . .

and sound travels at more than 680 miles per hour!

1 Air flowing over wings will lift a plane upward. But it will only do this if the plane is moving forward. This is what engines are for — to produce a strong forward force called thrust.

2 The faster the plane, the more powerful an engine it has. Heavy planes need more powerful engines, too — and usually more than one.

Engine

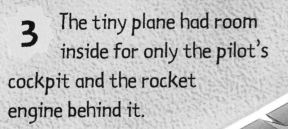

3 The tiny plane had room inside for only the pilot's cockpit and the rocket engine behind it.

4 The pilot's name was Chuck Yeager, and on October 14, 1947, he became the world's first supersonic human.

5 By 1953, jet engines were also powerful enough to take airplanes to supersonic speeds. Nowadays, many jet fighters fly at over twice the speed of sound. But only one jet airliner does — the Concorde.

3 Many planes now have jet engines, and the most common kind has a big fan at the front. As the fan spins, it sucks air into the engine, where it's burned with jet fuel. This creates a blast of hot gases, which roars out of the back of the engine and pushes the plane forward.

Cold air in

Hot gases out

4 Rocket engines give the most thrust. They're similar to jet engines, but they burn fuel with other chemicals instead of air. Very few planes have them, though, because they're expensive, noisy, and use lots of fuel!

ENGINES 11

LOOK, NO ENGINE!

1 All airplanes have wings, but they don't all have engines. How do they fly without them? Well, one way is to use human power instead of engine power.

2 In 1979, American cyclist Bryan Allen puffed, panted, and pedaled this strange-looking plane across the English Channel from England to France.

3 The plane's name is the Gossamer Albatross, and it's really a flying bicycle.

4 The pilot pedals like mad to turn a bike chain. The chain turns the propeller at the back, and the spinning propeller pushes the plane along.

Gossamer Albatross

5 Allen's Channel crossing was the world's first long-distance human-powered flight.

It wasn't fast, though — his 22-mile trip took 2 hours and 49 minutes!

6 Pedal power makes the Albatross fly only because the plane is so light. The whole thing weighs less than the pilot!

1 Gliders are planes without an engine. They can't take off by themselves, so they're towed up by a propeller plane. Once the glider is airborne, it lets the towline go.

2 Gliders have amazingly long wings, which give lots of lift. But without an engine, a glider can't reach the speed needed to get enough lift to stay up in the sky. It will slowly sink toward the ground, unless . . .

3 the pilot finds a gust of wind to carry the glider upward or catches a ride on some rising hot air — a thermal.

4 With plenty of wind and thermals, a skillful pilot can swoop and soar across the sky all day — just like the birds!

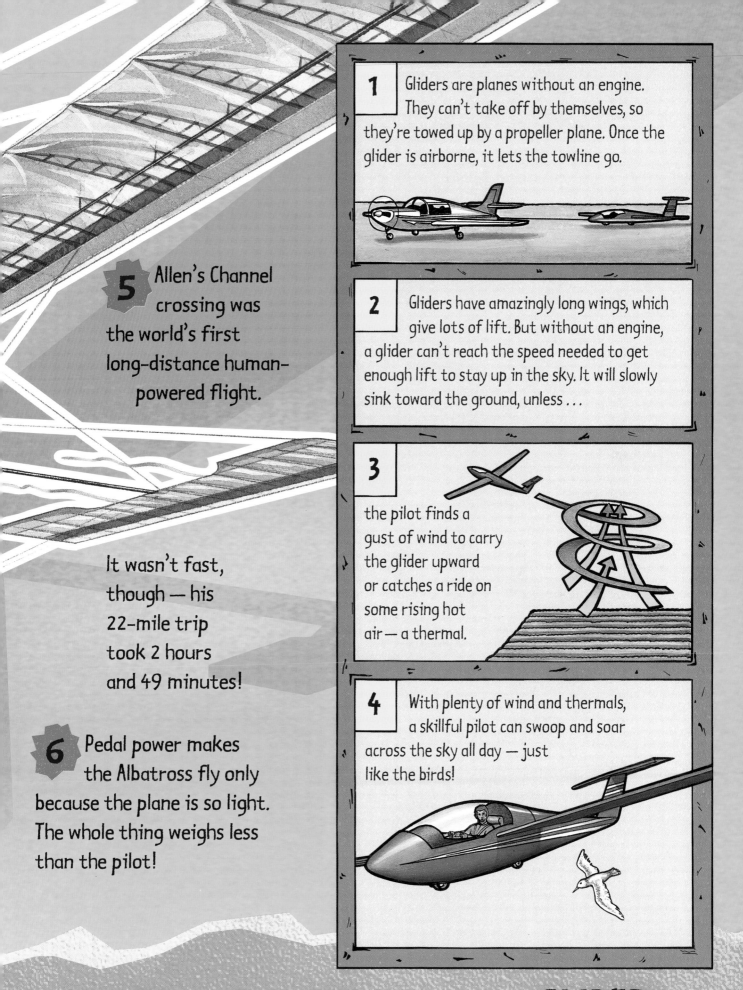

GLIDERS 13

GOING TO WORK

1 A plane with a broken nose? No, the front of this aircraft swings upward on massive hinges. It's a huge door into the airplane's main body, the fuselage.

3 Cargo planes carry all kinds of loads around the world — everything from airmail to flowers, racehorses to bulldozers.

2 This is an An-124, and it has almost twice as much room in its fuselage as a jumbo jet does. It doesn't have any seats, though, as it doesn't have any passengers — its job is carrying cargo.

14 CARGO PLANES

1 A fire has broken out in the middle of a forest, far from the nearest town. It would take a fire engine hours to reach the scene — but a fire plane can be there within minutes.

2 As the CL-415 Firebird swoops low over the flames, doors open under its fuselage. Out pours enough water to fill 100 bathtubs.

Doors

4 But when there's a disaster, such as an earthquake or a flood, cargo planes can rush in medicine and other emergency aid.

3 The Firebird needs more water, so it zooms off to a nearby lake. As the plane skims the lake's surface, water is forced through the fuselage doors into special storage tanks.

5 One single An-124 can fly in as much as four truckloads of supplies to a disaster area and carry away 500 people to safety.

4 Within minutes the Firebird is back over the forest, water bombing the flames again. After a few more trips, the fire will be out — good news for the forest plants and animals!

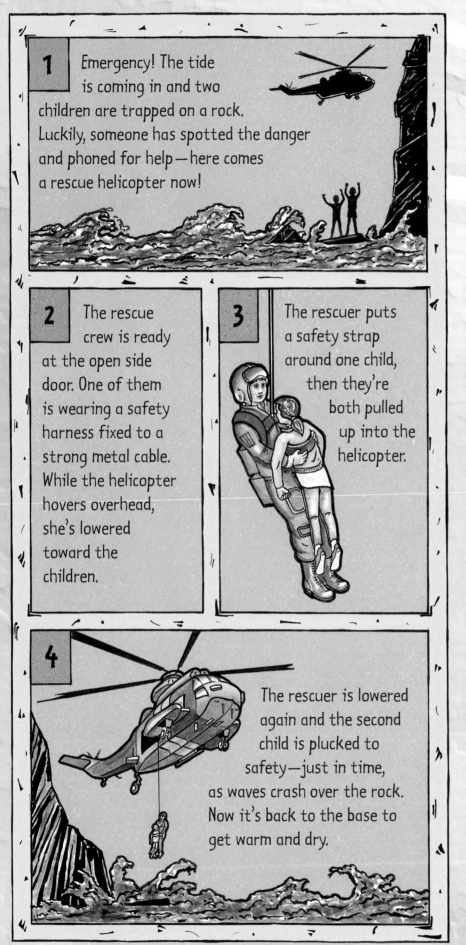

1 Emergency! The tide is coming in and two children are trapped on a rock. Luckily, someone has spotted the danger and phoned for help—here comes a rescue helicopter now!

2 The rescue crew is ready at the open side door. One of them is wearing a safety harness fixed to a strong metal cable. While the helicopter hovers overhead, she's lowered toward the children.

3 The rescuer puts a safety strap around one child, then they're both pulled up into the helicopter.

4 The rescuer is lowered again and the second child is plucked to safety—just in time, as waves crash over the rock. Now it's back to the base to get warm and dry.

1 Helicopters are often called choppers because they make such a loud chopping sound. The noise comes from the long blades on top of the helicopter slicing through the air.

2 The blades are called rotors, and each one is really a whirling wing — longer and narrower than an airplane wing, but still curved on top and flat underneath.

16 HELICOPTERS

GOING CHOPPING

4 If it had rotors only on top, the whole helicopter would spin around. The tail rotors stop this by turning in another direction.

5 Most planes only fly forward and need runways for taking off and landing. But helicopters can go straight up or down, sideways, backward, and even hover in one place.

6 Because they can go where normal aircraft can't, helicopters are used for special jobs—such as rescuing people or chasing criminals.

3 As the rotors whiz through the air, they create the sucking force called lift — just as airplane wings do.

HIDE-AND-SEEK

1 This F-117 Nighthawk fighter plane is on a spying mission. Its weird shape makes it invisible to the enemy—but how?

2 Most planes can be "seen" from the ground by radar, even at night. They show up as blips of light on special screens. But the Nighthawk doesn't!

1 How do pilots see where they're going in the middle of the night or when flying through thick clouds?

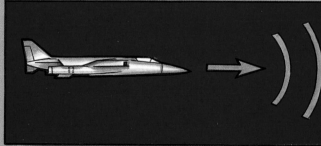

2 They use radar to "see" for them. The plane's radar equipment sends out invisible radio signals . . .

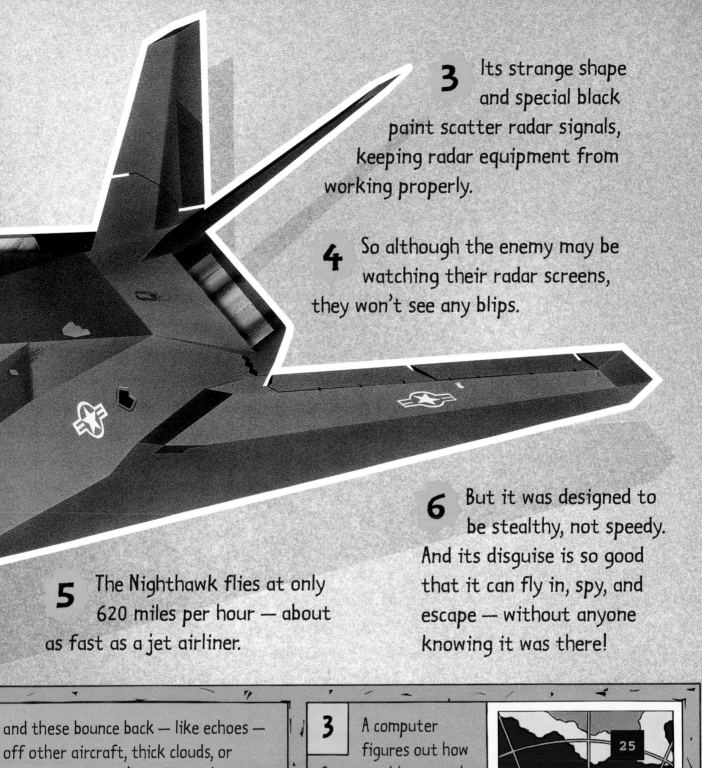

3 Its strange shape and special black paint scatter radar signals, keeping radar equipment from working properly.

4 So although the enemy may be watching their radar screens, they won't see any blips.

6 But it was designed to be stealthy, not speedy. And its disguise is so good that it can fly in, spy, and escape — without anyone knowing it was there!

5 The Nighthawk flies at only 620 miles per hour — about as fast as a jet airliner.

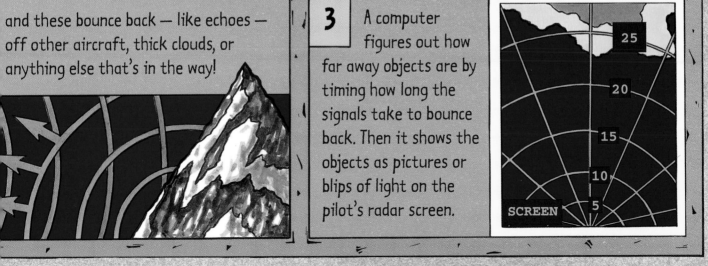

and these bounce back — like echoes — off other aircraft, thick clouds, or anything else that's in the way!

3 A computer figures out how far away objects are by timing how long the signals take to bounce back. Then it shows the objects as pictures or blips of light on the pilot's radar screen.

25
20
15
10
5
SCREEN

1 The world's very first air passenger was named Charlie Furnace. He worked with the Wright brothers, who built and flew the first powered aircraft in 1903. Orville Wright took a terrified Charlie up for a ride in 1908.

2 The first passenger planes flew in the 1920s. They were old propeller-driven bombers from World War I and were so cold and uncomfortable that passengers were given hot-water bottles to cuddle.

3 By the 1930s, passenger planes had heaters, padded chairs, and even reading lights. But their engines weren't powerful enough to fly above clouds and stormy weather, so flights could be very bumpy.

4 By the 1950s, planes had jet engines and were able to fly much faster and higher. This made journeys much quicker — and smoother, so fewer people got airsick!

5 Modern jet airliners fly 6 miles or more above the ground and cruise along at about 620 miles per hour — six times faster than the planes of the 1920s.

20 AIRLINERS

RIDE IN THE SKY

1 This Boeing 777 landed 20 minutes ago. Already, all 370 passengers have gone through the jetway into the airport building. Even so, the airliner is far from empty and quiet.

2 It's turnaround time. The plane must be checked, cleaned, refueled, reloaded, and ready to take off with new passengers in less than an hour.

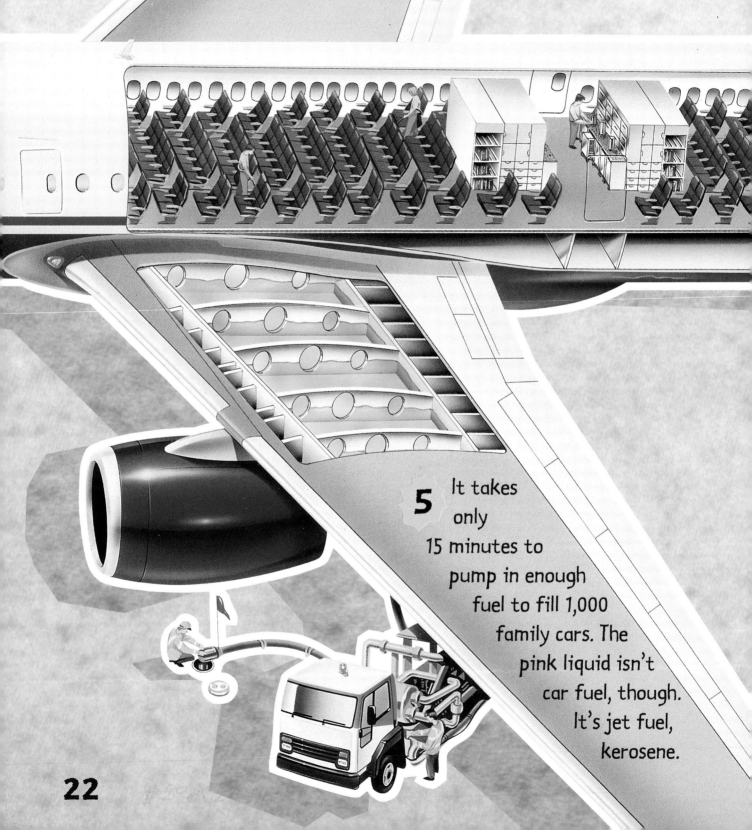

3 The ground crew is connecting pipes so the plane can be refueled.

4 The pipes join an underground storage tank to the plane's main fuel tanks, in the wings.

5 It takes only 15 minutes to pump in enough fuel to fill 1,000 family cars. The pink liquid isn't car fuel, though. It's jet fuel, kerosene.

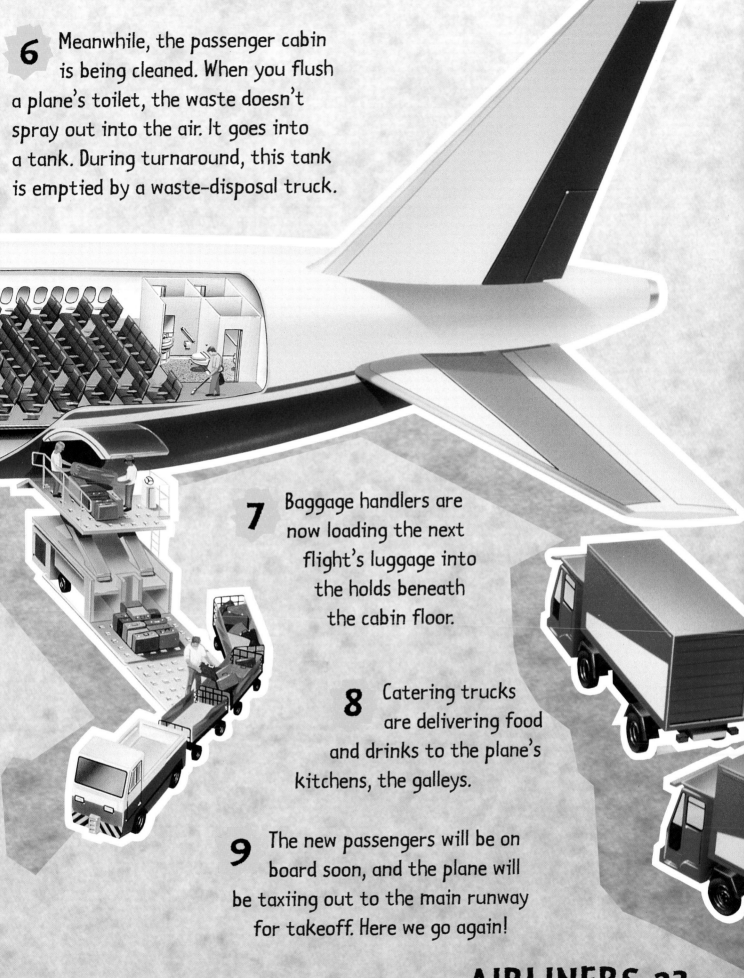

6 Meanwhile, the passenger cabin is being cleaned. When you flush a plane's toilet, the waste doesn't spray out into the air. It goes into a tank. During turnaround, this tank is emptied by a waste-disposal truck.

7 Baggage handlers are now loading the next flight's luggage into the holds beneath the cabin floor.

8 Catering trucks are delivering food and drinks to the plane's kitchens, the galleys.

9 The new passengers will be on board soon, and the plane will be taxiing out to the main runway for takeoff. Here we go again!

INDEX

Main illustrations by Andy Burton (18–19, 21–23); Roger Goode (cover; 8–9, 10–11, 22–23 cutaway);
Mike Lister (3, 5 main a/w); Darren Pattenden (4–5); Richard Morris (14–15); Tim Taylor (6–7, 15
inset); Darrell Warner (2, 12–13, 16–17); inset and picture-strip illustrations by Ian Thompson
With thanks to Beehive Illustration, Folio, and Helicopter Graphix
Designed by Jonathan Hair and Matthew Lilly; edited by Jackie Gaff and Paul Harrison
Text copyright © 1997 by Steve Parker
Illustrations copyright © 1997 by Walker Books Ltd.
All rights reserved.
First U.S. paperback edition 1998
Library of Congress Cataloging-in-Publication Data is available.
Library of Congress Catalog Card Number 96-34408
ISBN 0-7636-0128-4 (hardcover)
ISBN 0-7636-0631-6 (paperback)
2 4 6 8 10 9 7 5 3 1
Printed in Hong Kong
This book was typeset in Kosmik.
Candlewick Press
2067 Massachusetts Avenue
Cambridge, Massachusetts 02140

#39682034

QUIZ ANSWERS

Page 2—FALSE
A Portuguese priest, Father Gusmao, made a model hot-air balloon and flew it in 1709.

Page 6—FALSE
The helium gas is protected in big bags called cells. These are inside the airship's envelope.

Page 9—TRUE
They're called triplanes. Some early planes had up to nine pairs of wings!

Page 10—FALSE
The first rocket planes flew in the 1930s.

Page 12—TRUE
The space shuttle flies into space using rockets, but glides back down to Earth.

Page 14—FALSE
Its 226-foot-long fuselage makes the An-124 the second biggest. A stretched version, the An-225, has a 253-foot-long fuselage and is the world's largest plane.

Page 17—TRUE
But not all helicopters can loop the loop—only the latest designs, such as the Lynx.

Page 18—FALSE
Radar was invented in 1935 and first used in planes in the 1940s.

Page 20—TRUE
The captain or the copilot usually takes the controls for takeoff and landing, but the autopilot (a computer) often flies the plane at other times.